Health & Hygiene

T0363276

Seven steps to avoid food poisoning

Food safety in our home and workplace

KYLIE IRVING

Published in Australia by Sid Harta Publishers Pty Ltd,

ABN: 46 119 415 842

23 Stirling Crescent, Glen Waverley, Victoria 3150 Australia

Telephone: +61 3 9560 9920, Facsimile: +61 3 9545 1742

E-mail: author@sidharta.com.au

First published in Australia 2016

This edition published 2016

Copyright © Kylie Irving in 2016

Cover design, typesetting: WorkingType (www.workingtype.com.au)

The right of Kylie Irving to be identified as the Author of the Work has been asserted in accordance with the Copyright, Designs and Patents Act 1988.

All rights reserved. No part of this publication may be reproduced, stored in a retrieval system, or transmitted, in any form or by any means without the prior written permission of the publisher, nor be otherwise circulated in any form of binding or cover other than that in which it is published and without a similar condition being imposed on the subsequent purchaser.

Irving, Kylie

Health and Hygiene —7 steps to avoid food poisoning

ISBN: 978-1-877059-90-2

pp28

*I dedicate this book to
my daughters Bianca and Cassandra.*

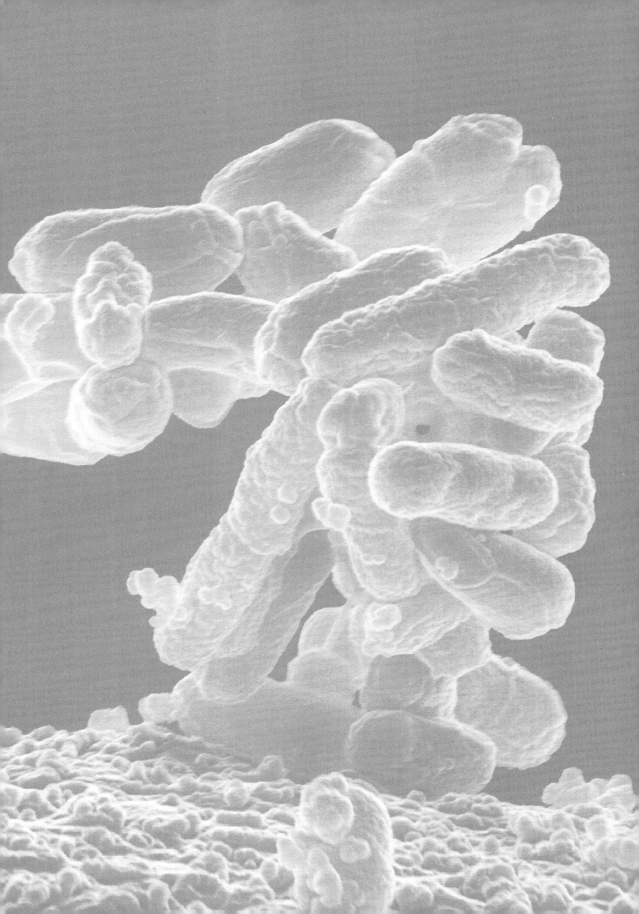

CONTENTS

Steps	Page

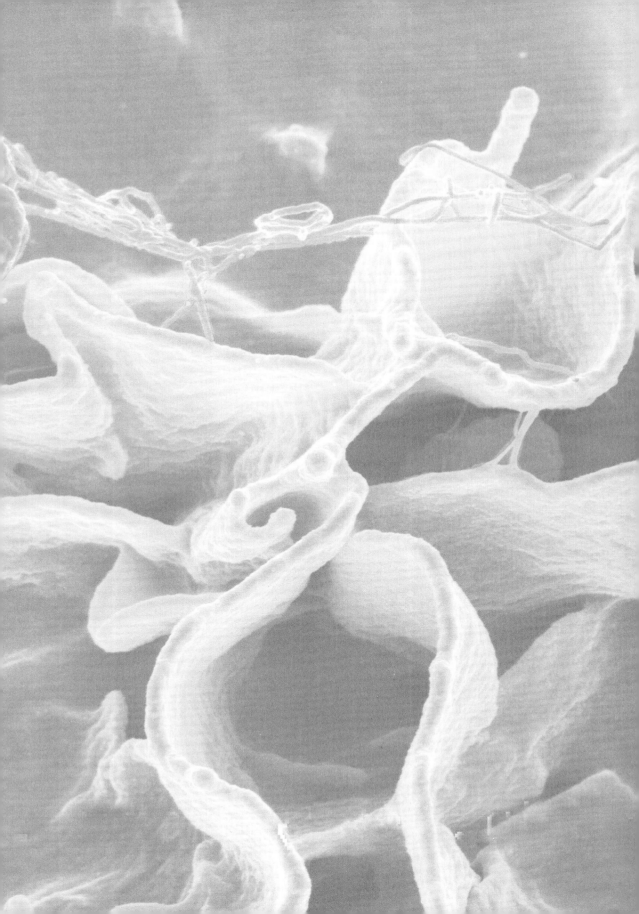

Introduction

Bacteria

We've used the term 'bacteria' to refer to the micro-organisms that grow on food and can infect anyone who eats these affected foods. It can take just seven hours for a single bacterium to multiply into more than two million bacteria. We cannot see bacteria, and it's not always the last thing that we eat that causes illness.

Bacteria lives in and on our bodies, especially on our hands. It can be transferred by hands, utensils, surfaces and wooden chopping boards if not cleaned properly. Bacteria generally grows well on foods that are warm and moist, and if food is left out of the fridge for more than four hours this can cause food poisoning from multiplying micro-organisms.

Bacteria is the most common cause of food poisoning, but it can be naturally prevented in food and in the right conditions.

Food poisoning

Food poisoning is most often caused by bacteria from food that is poorly handled, stored or cooked. The food may actually look, taste and smell normal but still be no good.

Some people are more at risk to get food poisoning than others — especially young children, pregnant women and the elderly. Symptoms of food poisoning include nausea, stomach cramps, diarrhoea, fever and headaches. With food poisoning you can't see it, feel it, smell it or taste it. The effects of food poisoning can start from one hour up to seventy-two hours after eating contaminated food.

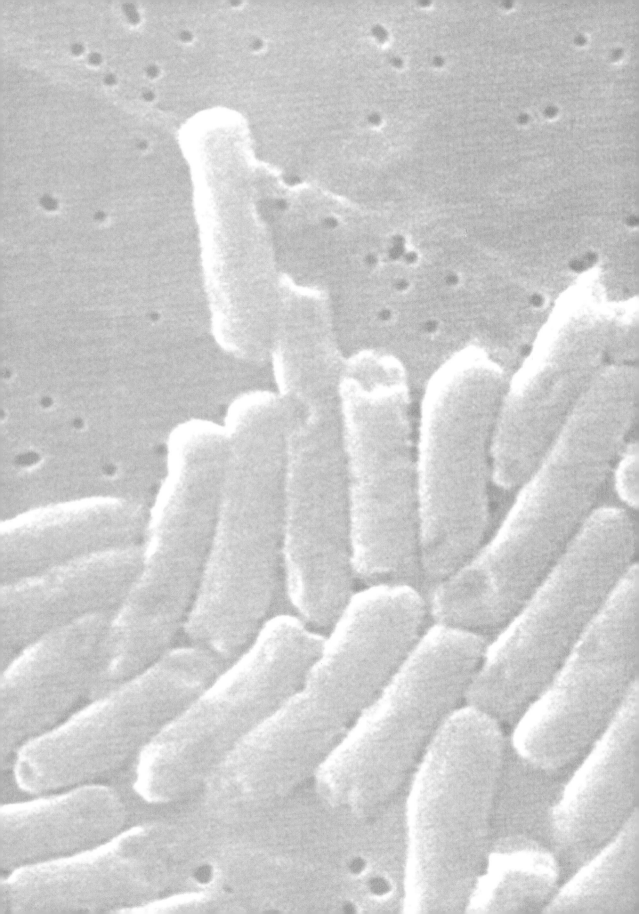

Step 1

High-risk foods

Meat: use the fridge to thaw frozen meat and chicken. Put frozen food on the bottom shelf of the fridge so that the blood doesn't drip on to other foods (to avoid cross-contamination). Use a sealed or covered container for storage. When defrosting food in the microwave, you must cook it straight away and have oil already hot in the frypan.

Poultry: cook poultry until meat is white; there should be no pink flesh or pink blood.

Dairy products: check the use-by dates and inspect for mould. Cream must not be out of the fridge for longer than two hours. The same rule applies for cakes with cream.

Cooked rice: leftovers must go in the fridge after you're finished eating.

Smallgoods: cold meat etc. must go in the fridge and be eaten within three to four days.

Eggs: don't use cracked eggs.

Seafood: store in the fridge. Fish should be cooked and eaten within three days.

Step 2

In the kitchen

To wipe down a table or kitchen bench, spray with water and a little bit of vinegar and wipe with a damp cloth; vinegar can help kill germs.

Don't stand near the microwave when it is on. The microwave should be cleaned after every use. No cling wrap or foil on the food in the microwave.

Clean out food in the fridge twice a week and clean the fridge thoroughly every two weeks.

Just because your dishcloths looks clean, that doesn't mean that they are; you must replace cloths at least every two weeks.

In the home, wooden chopping boards are preferable because more bacteria can sit on plastic boards. To clean a wooden chopping board, scrub it after every use with dishwashing liquid and rinse with water.

Clean up raw meat and raw chicken before going on to the next task. You must not thaw and then refreeze frozen food. Raw food and cooked food must be stored separately, to avoid cross-contamination.

Step 3

At the supermarket

At the supermarket you have to check the use-by dates, especially on meat and dairy.

If you buy meat and dairy products you must take them home within one hour. If the weather is hot you must take them home straight away. Make sure meat products are packed separately for other groceries.

Check for mould on foods such as cheese, crumpets and bread. Do not buy the product if you find mould on it.

Do not buy cans that are swollen or badly dented.

Frozen chicken that is slightly soft to touch has already begun to thaw, so you should not buy it.

Step 4

Out and about

Never buy cooked fish in a shopping centre, because you do not know how long it has been sitting there. It is best to buy it from a fish and chip shop.

Avoid hot food that is not steaming hot at places like the footy, canteens, festivals and fetes. Don't buy unrefrigerated sandwiches.

After eating fish and chips or anything greasy you must wash your hands (or use wipes). Do not put greasy fingers on the lip of your cup. Do not share your drinks; if it is shared it becomes cross-contaminated. Do not put food on tables; put a napkin down first (how clean are the tables?).

Any leftover food must be put into the fridge as soon as you have finished eating, so you can eat it the next day (pizza, Chinese food etc.) Do this within two hours.

When we go out sometimes, we get very hungry and we eat just about anything — but think before you eat it. How long has it been sitting out? Two hours or more can cause food poisoning from the bacteria on the food.

Step 5

Preparing for a barbecue

You must wash your hands before handling food. If you are preparing raw meat, then a salad, wash your hands after the raw meat. Always wash the chopping board and the area you're working in, such as all benches — then you can start preparing your salad.

Do not use the same set of tongs for different types of food. Salads and meat should use different tongs. Do not use the same utensils for raw meat and cooked meat.

Thoroughly cook all meat. Hamburgers and chicken must not have any pink bits in them.

The host's responsibility is to cover leftover cold food and cooked meat. Rice and salads should be placed in the fridge within two hours to avoid food poisoning. Guests sometimes arrive late.

Step 6

At the workplace

Cleaning takes place first and involves the physical removal of dirt from the surface; the process of sanitising is used after the cleaning phase to kill the bacteria we cannot see. A full clean is as follows:

1. **Pre-clean:** remove all dirt and food scraps from surfaces.

2. **Wash:** with water and detergent.

3. **Rinse:** wash the surface with clean water, then remove access water.

4. **Sanitise:** spray surfaces with a fine mist of sanitisers. These kill and control the growth of micro-organisms.

5. **Air dry:** allow surface to air dry.

If utensils touch the floor, they must be disposed of or re-washed. Don't handle glasses or cups anywhere near the drinking edge. Utensils, plates and trays that are coughed or sneezed on should be rewashed. Crockery shouldn't be chipped or cracked.

The reason to keep the kitchen clean is to prevent contamination of food. You should wipe down walls before benches, then finish off with floors. Cleaning as you go, making sure everything is clean before moving on to the next task is a critical step in preventing food poisoning.

Never touch cooked food with gloves on — if possible, use utensils such as tongs. Change gloves between handling dirty and clean areas. The same gloves shouldn't handle food then other items (e.g. money).

Step 7

Important tips

- Keep fridge clean of mould around seals.

- Raw food must be on the bottom shelf to avoid cross-contamination.

- Use two sets of tongs when cooking large amounts of meat — one for cooked meat and one for raw meat — to avoid cross contamination.

- Wash your hands regularly.

- Never touch cooked food with hands — use clean utensils. If tasting with a spoon, do not put the same spoon back into the food as this causes cross-contamination.

- When gardening and using potting mixture and soil, you must wash your hands straight away. You can get very sick from the bacteria in the potting mixture.

- Tomato sauce, soy sauce and mayonnaise must be placed in the fridge after opening them.

- Avoid food that is not steaming hot.

- Opened cans of food must not go into the fridge. Put it in a bowl with cling wrap or a tight-seal container.

- After touching any animals, you must wash your hands before eating (animals carry bacteria — especially reptiles)

- Do not give leftover food to animals on your plate.

- Use separate kitchen boards to cut up animal food; one for your use and one for the animals' use.

- Never wear aprons into the toilet.

- Wash your hands after changing from raw food to cooked food.

- Wash raw fruits and vegetables before cooking or eating to wash away the dirt.

- Always wash knives after every use.

- Bacteria is found almost everywhere. All food usually has at least some bacteria — take all precautions to keep bacteria levels down and you'll avoid severe food poisoning.

Author's Note

The inspiration for this booklet came about through wanting to teach my daughters to be safe with food. Safety can come in many forms and this book is intended to direct the safe use of food handling. It has taken me many years to obtain the confidence to finally put my knowledge into a resource that others can use. Food handling is not complicated; it is common sense, but we all need to be reminded to be sensible on occasion.

New Releases... also from Sid Harta Publishers

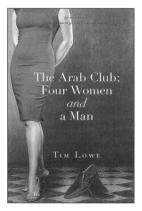

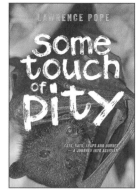

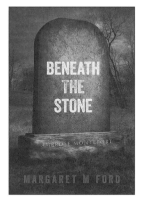

OTHER BEST SELLING SID HARTA TITLES CAN BE FOUND AT

http://sidharta.com.au   http://Anzac.sidharta.com

***

HAVE YOU WRITTEN A STORY?

http://publisher-guidelines.com

New Releases… also from Sid Harta Publishers

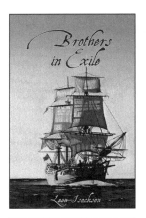

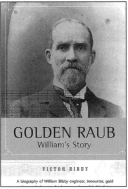

OTHER BEST SELLING SID HARTA TITLES CAN BE FOUND AT

http://sidharta.com.au   http://Anzac.sidharta.com

***

HAVE YOU WRITTEN A STORY?
http://publisher-guidelines.com

Best-selling titles by Kerry B. Collison

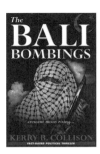   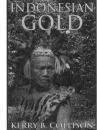

SID HARTA
PUBLISHERS

Readers are invited to visit our publishing websites at:
http://sidharta.com.au
http://publisher-guidelines.com/
Kerry B. Collison's home pages:
http://www.authorsden.com/visit/author.
asp?AuthorID=2239
http://www.expat.or.id/sponsors/collison.html
email: author@sidharta.com.au

Purchase Sid Harta titles online at:
http://sidharta.com.au

New Releases... also from Sid Harta Publishers

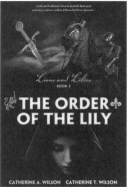

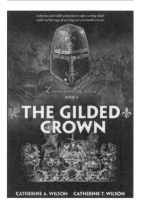

OTHER BEST SELLING SID HARTA TITLES CAN BE FOUND AT

http://sidharta.com.au   http://Anzac.sidharta.com

***

HAVE YOU WRITTEN A STORY?
http://publisher-guidelines.com